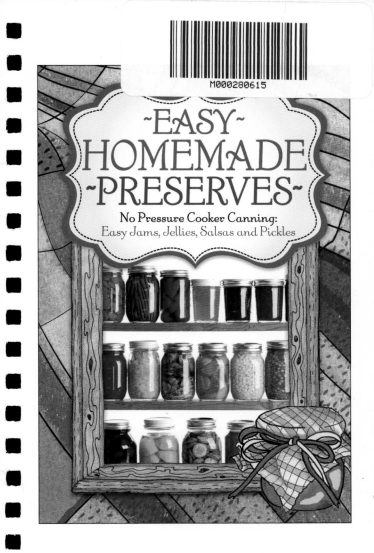

~EASY~ HOMEMADE ~PRESERVES~

No Pressure Cooker Canning:
Easy Jams, Jellies, Salsas and Pickles

Helen Hughes Hawkins

Cookbook Resources, LLC
Highland Village, Texas

Easy Homemade Preserves
No Pressure Cooker Canning: Easy Jams, Jellies,
Salsas and Pickles

Printed September 2012

International Standard Book Number: 978-1-59769-106-2

Library of Congress Control Number: 2011023540

Library of Congress Cataloging-in-Publication Data

      Hawkins, Helen Hughes.
       Easy homemade preserves : no pressure cooker
    canning : easy jams, jellies, salsas, and pickles / Helen
    Hughes Hawkins.
       p. cm.
     Includes bibliographical references and index.
     ISBN 978-1-59769-106-2
     1. Jam. 2. Jelly. I. Cookbook Resources, LLC. II.
    Title.
     TX612.J3H39 2011
     641.8'52--dc23
                             2011023540

Cover and design by Rasor Design

Edited, Designed and Published in the United States of America
and Manufactured in China by
Cookbook Resources, LLC
541 Doubletree Drive
Highland Village, Texas 75077

Toll free 866-229-2665

www.cookbookresources.com

Bringing Family and Friends to the Table

Easy Homemade Preserves

The best fruits and vegetables come from our own backyards and farmers' fields outside of town. No one will argue with that statement and more and more people are turning to locally grown fresh produce. Not only are the flavors better, but we know where our food comes from.

I remember learning to drive on the dirt road leading to the strawberry lady's house. Every summer we made regular trips there to pick our own strawberries. All year long we'd enjoy jams and jellies Mother made and it was one of those memories I'll never forget.

Easy Homemade Preserves is a very basic cookbook that will help you get started canning and preserving. It is not a textbook or reference book, but it is a good starting point for the benefits of sustainable lifestyles and locally grown produce.

It just makes sense to know where your food comes from, to get the most nutrition from home-grown produce and to get the most for your food dollars. But, the greatest value home canning and preserving may provide are the memories that last a lifetime and bring families together.

The best memories are made in the kitchen.

–The Editor

Contents

Recipes

Contents

Recipes - continued

Contents

Recipes - continued

Preserving Without a Pressure Cooker

The last time I saw my mother with a pressure cooker was the day it exploded. Canning went out with a bang in our household, but canning is safer and easier today. You don't have to use a pressure cooker to preserve all fruits and vegetables.

Although it takes a little time, preserving food today takes less than half the time it used to take and you don't need as much equipment or effort. That's a pretty good deal for the rewards you get.

Equipment

- Water canner with rack for jars*

- Tongs to lift jars

- Wide-mouth canning jars for whole fruits and vegetables

- Regular canning jars for salsas, sliced fruits and vegetables

- Rubber seal lids and screw-on rings

- Towels

Continued next page...

- Large saucepan or soup pot

- Big spoon

TIP: *You don't have to have a large, flat-bottom*
water canner with rack to preserve foods,
but because it is made for this purpose, it
is easier to add and to remove jars with the
rack that comes with the canner.

If using a soup pot, be sure to put a towel in
the bottom to set jars on so they won't crack.
Also be sure to leave 1 to 2 inches between
jars so the boiling water can circulate
around them.

Sterilizing Jars and Lids

Sterilize all jars in the dishwasher
or boiling water just before
using. Air dry thoroughly
before adding food. Make
sure there are no chips,
cracks or nicks in the glass or
on the rims.

Sterilize rubber seal lids in
simmering water and dry just before placing on
the jars.

Boiling Water Bath Method

Instead of using a pressure cooker, you can
preserve food packed in jars by placing them in a
boiling water bath.

1 . Place jars with lids in rack of water canner and
place inside canner. Fill canner with water

to 1 to 2 inches above tops of jars and remove rack with jars. Mark water line after rack is removed. This is amount of water needed to cover jars after they have been filled. Heat water to boiling. (It will take longer than you expect.)

2. Sterilize jars in boiling water in canner or in dishwasher and dry just before filling.

3. Fill hot jars with food and wipe rims clean. Tap jar on counter or press food down to remove all air bubbles. Loosely tighten rubber seal and screw-on ring.

4. Place in rack so that jars do not touch and water can circulate around the jars. Bring to a rolling boil, place lid on water canner and boil for the specified time.

(Add more boiling water if needed to make sure there is at least 1 inch above the jars. If boiling stops while processing, turn heat to highest setting and bring to a boil. Start timing again from the beginning.)

Continued next page...

All boiling times for water baths are for elevations at sea level to 1000 feet. Increase times at higher elevations.

Altitude (feet)	Increasing Processing Time
1000 - 3,000	Add 5 minutes to processing
3,001 - 6,000	Add 10 minutes to processing
6,001 - 8,000	Add 15 minutes to processing
8,001 - 10,000	Add 20 minutes to processing

5. Remove canner from heat and remove jars to cup towels on counter with at least 1 inch of space between them.

6. Let jars cool for about 24 hours. Test to make sure the seal is good on the jar. Press lid down; if it moves up and down, it is not sealed and contents should be refrigerated and used within a few days.

7. Label sealed jars with date and contents; use within 1 year.

What Foods Can Be Preserved with the Boiling Water Bath Method?

All high acid foods, such as most tomatoes, fruits, pickles, sauerkraut, jams, jellies and fruit butters can be preserved using the water bath method because the acidity or pH of these foods is lower than 4.6. Boiling water is enough to kill bacteria, molds, yeasts in most of these foods.

Important Notes

- Mason jars and screw-on rings can be washed and reused for years. Lids with the rubber seal cannot be reused because they will not seal properly a second time.

- Use canning (Mason) jars, not mayonnaise jars or other types. Canning jars are made of specially tempered glass to withstand the high temperatures needed for processing. Common brands of Mason jars include Kerr® and Ball®.

- Canner pot must have flat bottom and sit in center of heat source. Pot should not extend more than 4 inches past the heat source.

- Pickling salt (also called canning salt) is used throughout the recipes. It is fine-grained for easy dissolving and has no additives that can discolor preserved foods.

When Ready to Use the Product

Always recheck the seal when you are ready to use the product and refrigerate contents after opening. To check the seal, press the middle of the lid and if it springs back when released, discard the contents of the jar.

How Much Food to Buy for Preserving

(All amounts are approximate.)

Food	Amount	Canned Yields
Apples	8 medium apples (2¼ pounds)	1 (9 inch) pie or 3 cups applesauce
	2 large (1 pound)	3 cups sliced (1½ pints)
Apricots	1 pound	1 pint halved
Asparagus	3 - 4 pounds	1 quart stalks
Beets	3 pounds	1 quart whole
Berries (medium size)	1 pint	1 pint whole
Blueberries	1 pound	1 - 1½ pints
	3 pounds	1 quart
Cabbage	1 head (2 pounds)	8 cups, shredded (2 quarts)
Cherries	1 quart	1 quart with pits
Cucumbers	1 pound	1 - 1½ pints
Grapes	2 quarts	1 quart jelly
Green beans	1 pound	1 pint trimmed
Okra	1 pound	1 pint sliced
Onions	1 pound	1 pint chopped
Oranges	1 pound	1 cup juice or ½ pint sections

Food	Amount	Canned Yields
Peaches	1 pound	1 pint pureed or 1 - 1½ pints sliced
Pears	1 pound	1 pint
Peppers, sweet (bell)	1 pound	1½ - 2 pints chopped
Plums	2 pounds	1 quart
Strawberries	1 pint	1 pint whole or ½ pint pureed
	1 quart	1 pint pureed
Tomatoes	1 pound	½ - 1 pint peeled, chopped
	2 - 3 pounds	1 quart peeled, chopped

Two-piece lids as shown above are the best for long-term storage. Jars that are not sealed must be refrigerated.

Conversions by Volume

Amount	Converts to:
1 Gallon	4 quarts
	8 pints
1 Quart	2 pints
1 Pint	2 cups (16 fluid ounces)

Please note: Some photographs show products after they have been moved into serving jars or have lids other than proper sealing lids recommended for preserving. Any preserves not using proper canning jars and lids that seal must be refrigerated.

Basic Fruit Syrups

Light Syrup:

- Light syrup is used for small, soft fruits such as berries.

- Mix 1 cup sugar with 3 cups water and bring to a gentle boil; remove from heat and use while still very hot.

Medium Syrup:

- Medium syrup is used with peaches, apples, pears and sour or tart berries.

- Mix 1 cup sugar with 2 cups water and bring to a gentle boil; remove from heat and use while still very hot.

Heavy Syrup:

- Heavy syrup is used with sour or tart fruit – or if you want extra sweetness.

- Mix 1 cup sugar with 1 cup water and bring to a gentle boil; remove from heat and use while still very hot.

Apple Jelly

5 pounds apples, sliced
9 cups sugar
1 (32 ounce) and 1 (16 ounce) bottles apple
    juice
1 (1.7 ounce) box dry fruit pectin
1 teaspoon butter

- Place apples in large saucepan with about
  5 cups water and bring to a boil. Cover and
  simmer for about 15 minutes. Strain and
  mash apples through sieve or cheesecloth to
  separate peels, cores and seeds.

- Place strained apples in saucepan with
  remaining ingredients and bring to a
  rolling boil. Cook 1½ minutes and Pour
  into hot sterilized jars* to within ½ inch of
  top, wipe rims clean and screw on lids.

- Place jars in water bath** to cover and heat
  in boiling water for at least 10 minutes.
  Cool before tightening lids completely.
  Makes about 24 pints.

*Page 8: Instructions for sterilizing jars and lids.
**Page 8-10: Instructions for water bath.

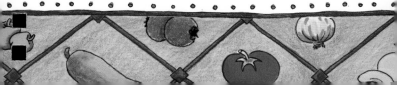

Apple Pie Apples

4 - 5 pounds apples, peeled, sliced
5 cups sugar
6 tablespoons tapioca

- Prepare enough apples to equal 12 cups sliced. Mix all ingredients with 3 cups water. Pour into hot sterilized jars* to within ½ inch of top, wipe rims clean and screw on lids.

- Place jars in water bath** to cover and heat in boiling water for at least 10 minutes. Cool before tightening lids completely. Makes enough for 4 pies.

*Page 8: Instructions for sterilizing jars and lids.
**Page 8-10: Instructions for water bath.

Hot water canning uses a canner or large pot with flat bottom and rack to hold jars. It is the best way to seal sterilized jars to prevent bacteria growth in food.

Apple Relish

5 medium onions, quartered
2 hot peppers, stemmed, seeded, halved
1 tablespoon pickling salt
14 large red apples with peels, cored, halved
1 quart vinegar
1 cup sugar
1 tablespoon pickling spice
1 tablespoon whole cloves
1 stick cinnamon

- Grate onions and peppers; add pickling salt and 1 cup boiling water. Let stand for 15 minutes in large saucepan and drain. Grate apples (with peels) and mix with onion mixture.

- Add vinegar, sugar and spices wrapped in cheesecloth to saucepan and cook on medium-high for 10 to 15 minutes. Pour into hot sterilized jars* to within ½ inch of top, wipe rims clean and screw on lids.

- Place jars in water bath** to cover and heat in boiling water for at least 10 minutes. Cool before tightening lids completely. Makes about 9 pints.

*Page 8: Instructions for sterilizing jars and lids.
**Page 8-10: Instructions for water bath.

Sassy Apple Butter

2½ - 3 pounds apples, peeled, cored, chopped
5 cups sugar
½ cup vinegar
1 (8 ounce) box Red Hots® cinnamon candy

- Process enough apples to equal 8 cups chopped and place in large saucepan. Add remaining ingredients, stir well and cook on medium-high for about 30 minutes; stir frequently.

- Pour into hot sterilized jars* to within ½ inch of top, wipe rims clean and screw on lids.

- Place jars in water bath** to cover and heat in boiling water for at least 10 minutes. Cool before tightening lids completely. Makes 6 pints.

*Page 8: Instructions for sterilizing jars and lids.
**Page 8-10: Instructions for water bath.

Gardening requires a lot of water…
most of it in the form of perspiration.
—Lou Erickson

Apricot Butter

4 pounds apricots, pitted, quartered
Honey

- Place apricots in large saucepan with ¼ cup water and cook over medium heat. Stir frequently and mash apricots as they soften. Continue mashing while cooking.

- Strain to remove peels. Return to heat and cook until it thickens. Sweeten with honey to taste. Pour into hot sterilized jars* to within ½ inch of top, wipe rims clean and screw on lids.

- Place jars in water bath** to cover and heat in boiling water for at least 10 minutes. Cool before tightening lids completely. Makes about 8 pints.

*Page 8: Instructions for sterilizing jars and lids.
**Page 8-10: Instructions for water bath.

After all is said and done, a lot
more is said than done.

—Murphy's Law

Dried Apricot Jam

1½ pints dried apricots
3¾ cups apple juice
2 lemons, juiced
3 cups sugar
¼ cup blanched, chopped almonds

- Soak apricots overnight in apple juice. Pour mixture into saucepan; add lemon juice and grated lemon peels (grate yellow part only). Bring to a boil and simmer for about 20 minutes.

- Add sugar, bring to a boil, stirring constantly, until sugar dissolves, about 20 minutes. Remove from heat and stir in almonds. Let stand for about 10 minutes. Pour into hot sterilized jars* to within ½ inch of top, wipe rims clean and screw on lids.

- Place jars in water bath** to cover and heat in boiling water for at least 10 minutes. Cool before tightening lids completely. Makes about 5 pints.

*Page 8: Instructions for sterilizing jars and lids.
**Page 8-10: Instructions for water bath.

Kickin' Apricot Preserves

5 pounds apricots, pitted
Juice of 1 lemon
1 (1.7 ounce) box fruit pectin
1 tablespoon butter
6 cups sugar
3 ounces amaretto liqueur

- Slice apricots into ½-inch pieces and cook in saucepan with 2 cups water until tender. Add lemon juice, pectin and butter, bring to a boil and remove from heat.

- Add sugar and bring back to a boil for 1 minute, stirring constantly. Remove from heat and add amaretto. Pour into hot sterilized jars* to within ½ inch of top, wipe rims clean and screw on lids.

- Place jars in water bath** to cover and heat in boiling water for at least 10 minutes. Cool before tightening lids completely. Makes about 5 to 6 pints.

*Page 8: Instructions for sterilizing jars and lids.
**Page 8-10: Instructions for water bath.

Pickled Asparagus Spears

1 pound fresh asparagus spears, trimmed
Garlic cloves
Dill weed
Cayenne pepper
2½ cups vinegar
¼ cup pickling salt

- Pack asparagus into sterilized* jars to
  within 1 inch of top. Add to each jar garlic,
  dill weed and cayenne pepper to taste.
  Bring vinegar, pickling salt and 2½ cups
  water to boil, pour over asparagus, wipe
  rims clean and screw on lids.

- Place jars in water bath** to cover and heat
  in boiling water for at least 10 minutes.
  Cool before tightening lids completely.
  Makes about 1 to 2 pints.

*Page 8: Instructions for sterilizing jars and lids.
**Page 8-10: Instructions for water bath.

Jars that are not sealed properly
must be refrigerated. (See page 10.)

Pickled Beets

15 pounds beetroot, peeled, trimmed
4 cups sugar
2 cups vinegar
1 teaspoon pickling spice

- Place enough beets in 5 sterilized* quart jars to within 1 inch of top. Combine 2 cups water with remaining ingredients in large saucepan and bring to rolling boil. Pour over beets. Wipe rims clean and screw on lids.

- Place jars in water bath** to cover and heat in boiling water for at least 10 minutes. Cool before tightening lids completely. Makes about 5 quarts.

*Page 8: Instructions for sterilizing jars and lids.
**Page 8-10: Instructions for water bath.

There are two types of canning: water bath canning and pressure-cooker canning. Water bath is the easiest and is featured exclusively in this cookbook.

Very Berry Jellies

*Almost any berry will work
with this recipe – so enjoy.*

**2 - 3 (1 quart) cartons ripe berries
3 cups sugar**

- Remove stems or leaves from berries
  and wash. Crush berries in large pot,
  add ¾ cup water and bring to a boil; stir
  frequently. Simmer for 5 minutes or until
  berries are soft.

- Let juice from berries drip through sieve or
  cheesecloth, but do not mash. (Jelly will be
  cloudy if crushed.) When you have 4 cups
  juice, discard cheesecloth and pulp and
  pour into large pot.

- Add sugar, bring to rolling boil and cook
  until mixture flows in sheets from metal
  spoon. Skim foam from top and Pour into
  hot sterilized jars* to within ½ inch of top,
  wipe rims clean and screw on lids.

- Place jars in water bath** to cover and heat
  in boiling water for at least 10 minutes.
  Cool before tightening lids completely.
  Makes about 3 to 4 pints.

*Page 8: Instructions for sterilizing jars and lids.
**Page 8-10: Instructions for water bath.

Pick of the Crop

Happy Chow-Chow

1 - 2 heads cabbage, shredded
2 - 2½ pounds tomatoes, minced
4 large onions, grated
4 bell peppers, cored, seeded, minced
2 - 4 jalapenos, seeded, minced
1 (16 ounce) bottle vinegar
4 cups sugar
2 tablespoons mustard seed
2 tablespoons celery seed
2 tablespoons turmeric

- Prepare enough shredded cabbage to equal 4 cups, enough minced tomatoes to equal 4 cups, enough grated onions to equal 4 cups, enough minced bell pepper to equal 4 cups. and enough minced jalapenos to equal 1 cup.

- Combine all ingredients in large saucepan, bring to a boil (may take 45 minutes), reduce heat and cook on low about 10 minutes. Pour into hot sterilized jars* to within ½ inch of top, wipe rims clean and screw on lids.

- Place jars in water bath** to cover and heat in boiling water for at least 10 minutes. Cool before tightening lids completely. Makes about 14 pints.

*Page 8: Instructions for sterilizing jars and lids.
**Page 8-10: Instructions for water bath.

Easy Sauerkraut

1 - 2 heads cabbage, shredded
2 teaspoons vinegar
1 teaspoon sugar
1 teaspoon pickling salt

- Place shredded cabbage loosely to within
  1 inch of top of sterilized* quart jar.
  Combine vinegar, sugar and pickling salt
  with 1 quart water in saucepan; bring
  to a boil.

- Pour hot liquid over cabbage and wipe rim
  clean. Tighten sterilized lid and ring on
  jar. Place in cold water bath for 30 minutes.

- When cool, press middle of lid. If it springs
  back, lid is not sealed and jar must be
  refrigerated. Store sealed jar in pantry
  for 6 weeks before serving. Makes about
  1 quart.

*Page 8: Instructions for sterilizing jars and lids.

No-Cook Carrot Relish

4 large carrots, chopped
9 red bell peppers, cored, seeded, sliced
9 yellow bell peppers, cored, seeded, sliced
2 heads cabbage, chopped
7 onions, sliced
½ cup pickling salt

- Mix above ingredients and let stand for 2 hours. Drain and rinse.

6 cups vinegar
4 cups sugar
2 tablespoons mustard seed
2 tablespoons celery seed

- Mix vinegar, sugar and seasonings; stir until sugar dissolves. Pack vegetables into sterilized jars* to within ½ inch of top. Pour vinegar mixture over vegetables, wipe rims clean and screw on lids.

- Place jars in water bath** to cover and heat in boiling water for at least 10 minutes. Cool before tightening lids completely. Makes about 16 pints.

*Page 8: Instructions for sterilizing jars and lids.
**Page 8-10: Instructions for water bath.

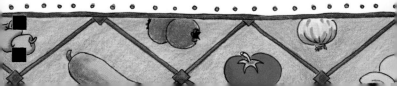

Homemade Cherry Jelly

6 - 6½ pounds cherries
1 (1.7 ounce) box fruit pectin
7 cups sugar

- Remove pits and puree enough cherries to equal 5 cups strained juice. Pour into saucepan with pectin and bring to rolling boil. Add sugar, bring back to a boil and cook for 1 to 1½ minutes.

- Pour into hot sterilized jars* to within ½ inch of top, wipe rims clean and screw on lids.

- Place jars in water bath** to cover and heat in boiling water for at least 10 minutes. Cool before tightening lids completely. Makes about 9 to 10 pints.

*Page 8: Instructions for sterilizing jars and lids.
**Page 8-10: Instructions for water bath.

Grandma's granddaughter's secret:
Wash and dry jars in dishwasher
before filling with food. It's easier
than washing in boiling water by hand.

Fresh Corn Relish

6 - 8 ears fresh corn
2 heads cabbage, shredded
4 - 5 large onions, chopped
2 - 3 pounds ripe tomatoes, peeled, chopped
1 - 2 pounds cucumbers, peeled, chopped
2 (16 ounce) bottles vinegar
2 cups sugar
1 tablespoon pickling salt
1 tablespoon celery seed
½ tablespoon turmeric

- Cut off enough corn kernels to equal 4 cups, shred enough cabbage to equal 4 cups, chop enough onion to equal 4 cups, chop enough tomatoes to equal 4 cups and chop enough cucumbers to equal 4 cups.

- Mix all ingredients to large saucepan and cook slowly for about 15 minutes. Pour into hot sterilized jars* to within ½ inch of top, wipe rims clean and screw on lids.

- Place jars in water bath** to cover and heat in boiling water for at least 10 minutes. Cool before tightening lids completely. Makes about 16 pints.

*Page 8: Instructions for sterilizing jars and lids.
**Page 8-10: Instructions for water bath.

Great Granny's Corncob Jelly

These red cobs make a pretty jelly.

12 red feeder corncobs, kernels stripped
1 (1.7 ounce) package dry fruit pectin
4 cups sugar

- Boil cobs in enough water to cover over medium high heat for about 20 minutes. Strain 3 cups liquid into large saucepan. Stir in pectin, bring to a boil and cook until mixture thickens.

- Add sugar and bring back to a boil for 1 minute. Pour into hot sterilized jars* to within ½ inch of top, wipe rims clean and screw on lids.

- Place jars in water bath** to cover and heat in boiling water for at least 10 minutes. Cool before tightening lids completely. Makes about 6 pints.

*Page 8: Instructions for sterilizing jars and lids.
**Page 8-10: Instructions for water bath.

Easy Winter Sweet Corn

This is an old Amish recipe used for years.

Corn-on-the-cob, shucked, silked*
Pickling salt
Sugar

- Cut corn off cobs into large bowl. Add a little pickling salt and a little sugar to taste and stir well. Pour into hot sterilized jars** to within ½ inch of top, wipe rims clean and screw on lids.

- Place jars in cold water in canner or flat-bottomed soup pot with towel padding inside. Cook on medium for about 3 hours. Store sealed jars in pantry.

*TIP: 1½ to 2 ears corn will equal about 1 cup kernels. 2 cups will fit into 1 pint jar.

**Page 8: Instructions for sterilizing jars and lids.

New gardeners learn by trowel and error.

Sweet Corn Relish

1 cup vinegar
½ cup sugar
1½ teaspoons mustard seed
½ teaspoon pickling salt
6 - 7 ears corn, shucked, silked
½ - 1 medium bell pepper, minced
½ small white onion, minced
1 (4 ounce) jar diced pimento
1 small rib celery, minced
1 clove garlic, minced

- Combine vinegar, sugar, mustard seed and pickling salt in large saucepan and boil for 2 minutes. Stir to dissolve sugar.

- Prepare enough corn kernels off cobs to equal 3½ cups, enough minced bell pepper to equal ½ cup and enough minced onion to equal ¼ cup.

- Add all ingredients to vinegar-sugar mixture and boil 3 minutes. Cool and refrigerate in airtight container. Makes 3 pints.

Jars that are not sealed properly must be refrigerated. (See page 10.)

Dill Pickles

Whole cucumbers
Vinegar
Fresh dill with seeds
2 (½ quart) bottles distilled water
1 (32 ounce) bottle vinegar
1 cup pickling salt

- Heat cucumbers in enough vinegar to cover and cook until cucumbers turn pale green. Drain vinegar and set aside for next batch.

- Pack cucumbers into sterilized quart or pint jars* to within 1 inch of top. Stuff 4 to 5 big stems fresh dill and 2 teaspoons dill seed into each quart jar. (Use half this amount for pint jars.)

- Mix distilled water, vinegar and salt, bring to a boil and pour over cucumbers to within ½ inch of top, wipe rims clean and screw on lids.

- Place jars in water bath** to cover and heat in boiling water for at least 10 minutes for pints and 15 minutes for quarts. Cool before tightening lids completely.

*Page 8: Instructions for sterilizing jars and lids.
**Page 8-10: Instructions for water bath.

Dandy Dills

10 pounds pickling cucumbers
5 medium onions
16 bay leaves
Fresh dill
Mustard seed
32 cloves garlic
32 small hot peppers
32 whole allspice berries
32 whole cloves
32 peppercorns
4 cups vinegar
1½ cups pickling salt

- Pack about 14 to 16 sterilized* pint jars with cucumbers, onions, 2 cloves garlic, 2 hot peppers, 1 bay leaf, dill, mustard seeds and 2 each of remaining seasonings.

- Bring 4 quarts water, vinegar and pickling salt to a boil in heavy saucepan. Pour into jars to within ½ inch of top, wipe rims clean and screw on lids.

- Place jars in water bath** to cover and heat in boiling water for at least 10 minutes. Cool before tightening lids completely. Makes about 16 pints.

*Page 8: Instructions for sterilizing jars and lids.
**Page 8-10: Instructions for water bath.

Gus's Garlic Pickles

10 - 15 pounds pickling cucumbers
Small hot peppers
Garlic cloves, peeled
1 cup vinegar
$\frac{1}{3}$ cup pickling salt
Fresh dill sprigs

- Pack cucumbers in sterilized* jars with
  1 pepper and 1 garlic clove in each jar.
  Bring 2 cups water, vinegar and pickling
  salt to a boil and fill sterilized jars* to
  within ½ inch of top.

- Place 1 or 2 dill sprigs on top of each jar,
  wipe rims clean and screw on lids.

- Place jars in water bath** to cover and heat
  in boiling water for at least 10 minutes.
  Cool before tightening lids completely.
  Pickles will be ready in about 3 weeks.

*Page 8: Instructions for sterilizing jars and lids.
**Page 8-10: Instructions for water bath.

No one is good at everything but
everyone is good at something.

Granny's Cucumber Pickles

7 pounds seedless cucumbers, peeled
2 cups pickling lime
1 (2 ounce) box powdered ginger

- Slice cucumbers lengthwise into spears.
  Dissolve lime in 2 gallons water, add
  spears and soak for 24 hours. Drain and
  thoroughly rinse 3 times. Mix ginger with
  2 gallons water, soak cucumbers in mixture
  for 6 hours and drain; do not rinse.

Brine:

5 pounds sugar
2 quarts vinegar
1 teaspoon celery seed
1 teaspoon allspice
1 teaspoon cloves

- Mix sugar and vinegar in large saucepan,
  stir to dissolve sugar and add spices. Add
  cucumbers and let stand for 1 hour. Bring

Continued next page…

Continued from previous page...

to a boil, reduce heat and cook slowly for 1 hour. Pack cucumbers into sterilized jars* to within ½ inch of top, pour brine over top, within ½ inch of top, wipe rims clean and screw on lids.

- Place jars in water bath** to cover and heat in boiling water for at least 10 minutes. Cool before tightening lids completely. Makes about 7 quarts.

*Page 8: Instructions for sterilizing jars and lids.
**Page 8-10: Instructions for water bath.

Peter Piper picked a peck of pickled peppers,

A peck of pickled peppers Peter Piper picked.

If Peter Piper picked a peck of pickled peppers,

Where's the peck of pickled peppers Peter Piper picked?

—Mother Goose

Annie B's Bread-and-Butter Pickles

My grandmother gave me this family recipe. It is more than 100 years old and still used today.

25 large cucumbers
12 onions
½ cup pickling salt
2 cups vinegar
2 cups sugar
2 tablespoons mustard seed
2 tablespoons turmeric
2 tablespoons ginger

- Soak cucumbers overnight in water. Slice cucumbers and onions, add pickling salt and let stand for 1 hour; rinse well.

- Mix vinegar, sugar, mustard seed, turmeric and ginger. Bring to a boil, add cucumbers and onions and boil for 40 minutes.

Continued next page...

Continued from previous page...

- Pour into hot sterilized jars* to within ½ inch of top, wipe rims clean and screw on lids.

- Place jars in water bath** to cover and heat in boiling water for at least 10 minutes. Cool before tightening lids completely. Makes about 10 to 12 pints.

*Page 8: Instructions for sterilizing jars and lids.
**Page 8-10: Instructions for water bath.

Annie B's Bread-and-Butter Pickles →

The best way to garden is to put on a wide-brimmed straw hat and some old clothes. Get a hoe in one hand and a cold drink in the other and tell someone else where to dig.

—Texas Bix Bender
Don't Throw in the Trowel

Quick Bread-and-Butter Pickles

1 quart jar whole dill pickles
1½ cups sugar
1 onion, sliced
2 cinnamon sticks
2 tablespoons vinegar

- Drain pickles and slice into large bowl; add all ingredients and mix well. Return to washed original jar and tighten lid.

- Let stand at room temperature for 4 to 5 days and turn jar upside down every other day. Store in refrigerator. Makes 1 quart.

Farmers are real experts. They are often outstanding in their fields.

Sweet Hot Pickles

1 (1 gallon) jar or 4 (1 quart) jars whole dill
   pickles, drained, rinsed
4 pounds sugar
6 cloves garlic, chopped
1 (5 ounce) bottle hot sauce

- Place rinsed and drained pickles in large
  pot. Add sugar, garlic and hot sauce and
  stir well.

- Pour into original 1-gallon jar or
  4 (1 quart) jars and let stand for 6 days in
  refrigerator. Turn jar upside down every
  day. After 6 days, the pickles are ready to
  serve. Store in refrigerator. Makes
  1 gallon or 4 quarts.

Pack vegetables and fruits tightly in
hot jars and pour hot or boiling syrup
or liquid to within $\frac{1}{2}$ inch of top. This
allows for food to expand and for a
proper seal to occur.

Fig Jam

1¼ - 1¾ pounds figs, seeded
1 (6 ounce) box lemon gelatin
3 cups sugar

- Crush enough figs to equal 3 cups. Bring
  all ingredients to a boil in saucepan, reduce
  heat and simmer for 10 minutes or until
  mixture thickens.

- Pour into hot sterilized jars* to within
  ½ inch of top, wipe rims clean and screw
  on lids.

- Place jars in water bath** to cover and heat
  in boiling water for at least 10 minutes.
  Cool before tightening lids completely.
  Makes about 3 pints.

*Page 8: Instructions for sterilizing jars and lids.
**Page 8-10: Instructions for water bath.

A perfect summer day is when the
sun is shining, the breeze is blowing,
the birds are singing and the lawn
mower is broken.
                                        —James Dent

Spiced Figs

6½ - 7 pounds firm, ripe figs
5 cups sugar, divided
3 cups vinegar
1 teaspoon whole cloves
1 tablespoon whole allspice berries
2 sticks cinnamon

- Peel or parboil figs to remove skins and pits; set aside to cool and drain. Add 3 cups sugar and 1½ quarts water to separate saucepan and cook on medium heat until sugar dissolves; stir occasionally. Add figs and simmer for 30 minutes.

- Add remaining sugar and vinegar. Tie spices in cloth bag and add to figs. Cook gently until figs are translucent. Cover and let stand for 12 to 24 hours in cool place. Remove spice bag; heat to simmer. Pour into hot sterilized jars* to within ½ inch of top, wipe rims clean and screw on lids.

- Place jars in water bath** to cover and heat in boiling water for at least 10 minutes. Cool before tightening lids completely. Makes about 8 pints.

*Page 8: Instructions for sterilizing jars and lids.
**Page 8-10: Instructions for water bath.

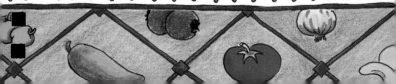

Grape Butter

1 gallon (8 - 9 pounds) grapes
Honey

- Place grapes in large saucepan or soup pot with ¼ cup water and cook over medium heat. Stir frequently and mash as grapes soften.

- Strain to remove skin and seeds. Return to heat and cook until thick. Add honey to sweeten. Pour into hot sterilized jars* to within ½ inch of top, wipe rims clean and screw on lids.

- Place jars in water bath** to cover and heat in boiling water for at least 10 minutes. Cool before tightening lids completely. Makes about 9 pints.

*Page 8: Instructions for sterilizing jars and lids.
**Page 8-10: Instructions for water bath.

A magical tractor was driving down
the road and turned into a field.

Homemade Grape Jelly

4 - 5 pounds very ripe seedless grapes
1 (1.7 ounce) box fruit pectin
7 cups sugar

- Mash enough grapes through sieve to equal 5 cups strained juice. (Add water if needed to make 5 cups.*) Pour into saucepan with pectin and bring to rolling boil. Add sugar, bring back to a boil and cook for 1 to 1½ minutes.

- Pour into hot sterilized jars** to within ½ inch of top, wipe rims clean and screw on lids.

- Place jars in water bath*** to cover and heat in boiling water for at least 10 minutes. Cool before tightening lids completely. Makes about 4 to 5 pints.

*TIP: *Very ripe grapes will make plenty of juice. Add no more than 1 cup water if necessary.*

**Page 8: Instructions for sterilizing jars and lids.
***Page 8-10: Instructions for water bath.

Pickled Green Beans

4 heads dill or 2 - 3 tablespoons dill seeds
4 cloves garlic, peeled
2 pounds fresh tender green beans
¼ cup pickling salt
2 cups vinegar

- Place dill head or seeds and garlic clove in each of 4 sterilized* pint jars. Snap ends of beans off and place in jars. Combine salt, vinegar and 2 cups water in saucepan and bring to a boil.

- Pour liquid into hot sterilized jars to within ½ inch of top, wipe rims clean and screw on lids.

- Place jars in water bath** to cover and heat in boiling water for at least 10 minutes. Cool before tightening lids completely. Makes about 4 pints.

*Page 8: Instructions for sterilizing jars and lids.
**Page 8-10: Instructions for water bath.

What do you call two recently married spiders?

Newly webs.

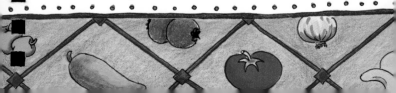

Party Pickled Okra

Small okra pods with stems, trimmed
Garlic cloves
Jalapenos
Vinegar

- Place okra, 2 cloves garlic and 1 jalapeno in each sterilized* pint jar.

- Bring equal amounts of water and vinegar to boil and pour into hot sterilized jars to within ½ inch of top, wipe rims clean and screw on lids.

- Place jars in water bath** to cover and heat in boiling water for at least 10 minutes. Cool before tightening lids completely. Store sealed jars in pantry for 3 weeks before serving.

*Page 8: Instructions for sterilizing jars and lids.
**Page 8-10: Instructions for water bath.

Life is not a dress rehearsal.

Onion Relish

This is a gorgeous amber color and is delicious.

3 - 4 pounds large white onions, diced
2 cups vinegar
2 cups sugar
1 teaspoon pickling salt

- Prepare enough diced onions to equal
  8 cups. Pour just enough boiling water over
  onions to cover and let stand 5 minutes.

- Pour vinegar, sugar and pickling salt in
  large saucepan, add onions and simmer for
  25 minutes. Pour into hot sterilized jars*
  to within ½ inch of top, wipe rims clean and
  screw on lids.

- Place jars in water bath** to cover and heat
  in boiling water for at least 10 minutes.
  Cool before tightening lids completely.
  Makes about 6 pints.

*Page 8: Instructions for sterilizing jars and lids.
**Page 8-10: Instructions for water bath.

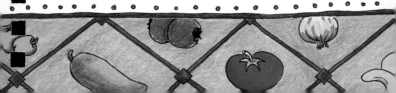

Orange Marmalade

4 - 5 oranges, peeled, sliced
3 - 4 lemons, peeled, sliced
Sugar

- Place fruit in large glass bowl and cover with 6 cups water. Let stand overnight. Pour mixture into saucepan and cook over medium-high heat about 30 minutes or until tender. Let stand overnight.

- On third day, add 2 cups sugar for each 1 pint of fruit. Cook fruit and sugar over medium heat until it reaches jelly consistency, about 10 minutes. Pour into hot sterilized jars* to within ½ inch of top, wipe rims clean and screw on lids.

- Place jars in water bath** to cover and heat in boiling water for at least 10 minutes. Cool before tightening lids completely. Makes about 7 pints.

*Page 8: Instructions for sterilizing jars and lids.
**Page 8-10: Instructions for water bath.

Where do apples like to go on vacation?
Fuji.

Brandied Cranberry-Orange Marmalade

2 cups fresh cranberries
1 cup brandy
⅔ cup orange juice
2 tablespoons grated orange peel

- Place cranberries in quart jar and pour brandy over top. Let stand for 48 hours and drain.

- Pour cranberries, orange juice and orange peel in large pot and bring to a boil. Reduce heat to low, stir occasionally, and cook about 15 minutes or until cranberries pop. Pour into hot sterilized jars* to within ½ inch of top, wipe rims clean and screw on lids.

- Place jars in water bath** to cover and heat in boiling water for at least 10 minutes. Cool before tightening lids completely. Makes about 1 pint.

*Page 8: Instructions for sterilizing jars and lids.
**Page 8-10: Instructions for water bath.

Peach Butter

4 pounds peaches, pitted

- Peel or parboil peaches to remove skin. Place in large saucepan with one-third amount of water to peaches. Simmer to soften peaches; stir frequently. Puree in food processor or blender.

- Pour into baking pan and bake, uncovered, at 325° for 1 hour. Remove from oven, stir well and continue to bake, stirring every 15 to 20 minutes, until mixture is thick and reddish amber color.

- Pour into hot sterilized jars* to within ½ inch of top, wipe rims clean and screw on lids.

- Place jars in water bath** to cover and heat in boiling water for at least 10 minutes. Cool before tightening lids completely. Makes about 8 to 10 pints.

*Page 8: Instructions for sterilizing jars and lids.
**Page 8-10: Instructions for water bath.

Brandied Peaches

9 cups sugar
2 cinnamon sticks
1 tablespoon whole cloves
5 pounds peaches, peeled, pitted, halved
1⅔ cups brandy

- Dissolve sugar in 2½ cups water. Place cinnamon and cloves in cheesecloth bag and add to water. Bring to a boil; add peaches a few at a time and cook until peaches are just tender.

- Place colander over bowl, drain peaches and save syrup. Bring syrup to a boil until it thickens slightly. Add brandy and stir. Pack peaches into sterilized jars* to within ½ inch of top. Pour syrup over top, wipe rims clean and screw on lids.

- Place jars in water bath** to cover and heat in boiling water for at least 10 minutes. Cool before tightening lids completely. Makes about 8 to 9 pints.

*Page 8: Instructions for sterilizing jars and lids.
**Page 8-10: Instructions for water bath.

Pickled Peaches

5 cups sugar
1¼ cups vinegar
¼ cup whole cloves
5 pounds small white clingstone peaches,
    peeled
8 (2 - 3 inch) cinnamon sticks
1 tablespoon nutmeg, optional

- Boil sugar, vinegar and 1¼ cups water in
  large pot for about 5 to 7 minutes to make
  syrup. Stick cloves into peaches and add
  to pot. Add cinnamon sticks and nutmeg
  wrapped in cheesecloth bag. Return syrup
  to boil and cook for about 25 minutes or
  until peaches are tender.

- Remove cinnamon sticks and nutmeg bag.
  Pour peaches and syrup into sterilized jars*
  to within 1 inch of top, wipe rims clean and
  screw on lids.

- Place jars in water bath** to cover and heat
  in boiling water for at least 10 minutes.
  Cool before tightening lids completely.
  Makes about 9 to 10 pints.

*Page 8: Instructions for sterilizing jars and lids.
**Page 8-10: Instructions for water bath.

Peach Preserves

1 - 1½ pounds (underripe) peaches
1½ - 2 cups sugar

- Peel and chop enough peaches to equal
  3 cups. Cook with ¼ cup water in large
  saucepan over medium heat, stirring
  frequently, for about 5 minutes or until
  barely tender.

- Drain juice into measuring cup and pour
  into second saucepan. Add 2 cups sugar for
  1 cup juice. Boil juice, stirring constantly,
  until sugar spins a thread.

- Add peaches and cook at rapid boil for
  4 to 5 minutes. Remove from heat; skim
  if necessary. Pour into hot sterilized jars*
  to within ½ inch of top, wipe rims clean
  and screw on lids.

- Place jars in water bath** to cover and heat
  in boiling water for at least 10 minutes.
  Cool before tightening lids completely.
  Makes about 1 pint.

*Page 8: Instructions for sterilizing jars and lids.
**Page 8-10: Instructions for water bath.

Pickled Pears

3 pounds pears, peeled
Juice of 2 lemons
1½ pounds sugar
4 cups cider vinegar
3 cinnamon sticks
3 star anise
1 teaspoon peppercorns
1 teaspoon allspice

- Toss pears with lemon juice. Place in large saucepan with remaining ingredients and bring to a boil. Reduce heat and cook until pears are tender. Spoon into sterilized* jars and pour syrup over top to within ½ inch of top, wipe rims clean and screw on lids.

- Place jars in water bath** to cover and heat in boiling water for at least 10 minutes. Cool before tightening lids completely. Makes about 3 to 4 quarts.

*Page 8: Instructions for sterilizing jars and lids.
**Page 8-10: Instructions for water bath.

Like a prune, we're not getting any better looking, but we are getting sweeter.

—N.D. Stice

Pear Honey

4 - 5 pounds ripe pears, peeled, cored
1 (8 ounce) can crushed pineapple
1 lemon, juiced
5 cups sugar

- Process enough pears to equal 9 cups puree and add to saucepan. Stir in pineapple, lemon juice and sugar. Grate only yellow peel of lemon and add to mixture. Cook on low for about 20 minutes.

- Pour into hot sterilized jars* to within ½ inch of top, wipe rims clean and screw on lids.

- Place jars in water bath** to cover and heat in boiling water for at least 10 minutes. Cool before tightening lids completely. Makes about 6 pints.

*Page 8: Instructions for sterilizing jars and lids.
**Page 8-10: Instructions for water bath.

A man should never plant a garden
larger than his wife can take care of.
—T.H. Everett

Pear Preserves

10 pounds pears, peeled, sliced
2 pounds sugar

- Place pears in large bowl, spread sugar over top and let stand, covered, overnight. In large saucepan, bring mixture to a boil, simmer and cook until syrup thickens, probably several hours.

- Pour into hot sterilized jars* to within ½ inch of top, wipe rims clean and screw on lids.

- Place jars in water bath** to cover and heat in boiling water for at least 10 minutes. Cool before tightening lids completely. Makes about 10 pints.

*Page 8: Instructions for sterilizing jars and lids.
**Page 8-10: Instructions for water bath.

If April showers bring May flowers,
what does a May flower bring?
Pilgrims

Jalapeno Sweet Pickles

1 (1 gallon) jar whole dill pickles
1 (16 ounce) jar sliced jalapenos with liquid
4 pounds sugar

- Drain and rinse pickles. Cut into ½-inch thick pieces and place in large pot. Add jalapeno with juices and sugar and stir well.

- Pour into original gallon jar and let stand for 6 days. Turn jar upside down every day. Store in refrigerator. Makes 1 gallon.

Never recycle jars from prepared foods (like mayonnaise or barbecue sauce, etc.) for canning because the glass will not withstand the temperatures used in canning. Only use jars, lids and seals made for canning. Never reuse rubber seals.

Fun Jalapeno Jelly

Great poured over cream cheese and served with crackers! It's terrific with all meats as well.

3 - 4 large jalapenos
3 small bell peppers, cored, seeded
1¼ cups vinegar
1 pouch liquid fruit pectin
6½ cups sugar

- Wear rubber gloves to stem, seed and mince enough jalapenos to equal ¾ cup and enough bell peppers to equal ¾ cup grated. Add all ingredients, except sugar, to saucepan and boil 5 minutes. Cool 20 minutes.

- Return to high heat and cook 2 minutes. Add sugar and cook 4 minutes. Pour into hot sterilized jars* to within ½ inch of top, wipe rims clean and screw on lids.

- Place jars in water bath** to cover and heat in boiling water for at least 10 minutes. Cool before tightening lids completely. Makes about 3 pints or 6 half-pints.

*Page 8: Instructions for sterilizing jars and lids.
**Page 8-10: Instructions for water bath.

Pick of the Crop

Dad's Favorite Jalapeno Relish

5 pounds jalapenos, cored, seeded, minced*
2 pounds onions, peeled, minced
4 - 5 pods garlic, separated into cloves,
    peeled, minced
½ cup sugar
1 (1 quart) bottle vinegar
¼ cup mustard seed
¼ cup pickling salt

- Mix all ingredients in large saucepan; cook
  over medium heat for 1 hour. Pour into hot
  sterilized jars* to within ½ inch of top, wipe
  rims clean and screw on lids.

- Place jars in water bath** to cover and heat
  in boiling water for at least 10 minutes.
  Cool before tightening lids completely.
  Makes about 6 pints.

*TIP: Wear rubber gloves when handling
      jalapenos and other hot peppers.

*Page 8: Instructions for sterilizing jars and lids.
**Page 8-10: Instructions for water bath.

Pickled Jalapeno Slices

Jalapenos, stemmed, seeded, sliced
Distilled vinegar
Olive oil
Pickling salt

- Stuff jalapenos, 1 tablespoon distilled vinegar, ½ teaspoon olive oil and ½ teaspoon pickling salt into each hot sterilized* pint jar. Pour boiling water over jalapenos to within ½ inch of top, wipe rims clean and screw on lids.

- Place jars in cold water bath for 35 minutes. When cool, press middle of lid. If it springs back, lid is not sealed and jar should be refrigerated. Store sealed jars in pantry.

*Page 8: Instructions for sterilizing jars and lids.

My wife's a water sign. I'm an earth sign.

Together we make mud.

—Rodney Dangerfield

Peter Piper's Pickled Peppers

2 teaspoons mustard seed, divided
2 teaspoons whole allspice, divided
2 teaspoons pickling salt, divided
2½ cups vinegar
½ cup sugar
6 green bell peppers, cored, seeded, quartered
6 red bell peppers, cored, seeded, quartered

- Place ½ teaspoon mustard seed, ½ teaspoon whole allspice and ½ teaspoon pickling salt in each of 4 sterilized pint jars*. Bring vinegar, sugar and 2½ cups water to a boil in large saucepan; add peppers and heat thoroughly.

- Pour into hot sterilized jars to within ½ inch of top, wipe rims clean and screw on lids. Place jars in water bath** to cover and heat in boiling water for at least 10 minutes. Cool before tightening lids completely. Makes about 4 pints.

TIP: Use this recipe for just about any kind of peppers... the peppers in the photograph are long green peppers similar to cayenne peppers before they turn red.

*Page 8: Instructions for sterilizing jars and lids.
**Page 8-10: Instructions for water bath.

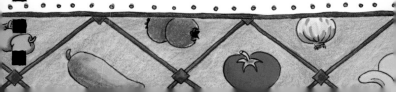

Sweet Pepper Relish

12 green bell peppers, cored, seeded, finely chopped
12 red bell peppers, cored, seeded, finely chopped
15 medium onions, finely chopped
4 cups vinegar
5 cups sugar
2 tablespoons pickling salt

- Place vegetables in large saucepan. Bring vinegar, sugar and pickling salt to a boil and pour over vegetables. Gently boil until peppers are tender (about 25 minutes).

- Pour into hot sterilized jars* to within ½ inch of top, wipe rims clean and screw on lids.

- Place jars in water bath** to cover and heat in boiling water for at least 10 minutes. Cool before tightening lids completely. Makes about 7 pints.

*Page 8: Instructions for sterilizing jars and lids.
**Page 8-10: Instructions for water bath.

Hot Pepper Relish

4 pounds green tomatoes, minced
4 large onions, minced
4 - 6 large jalapenos, seeded, minced
2 - 4 bell peppers, cored, seeded, minced
1 quart vinegar
2 cups sugar
1 cup prepared mustard

- Prepare enough minced tomatoes to equal
  4 cups, enough minced onion to equal
  4 cups, enough minced jalapenos to equal
  4 cups and enough minced bell pepper to
  equal 2 cups.

- Mix all ingredients in large saucepan and
  bring to a boil. Reduce heat to medium
  and cook for 10 minutes. Pour into hot
  sterilized jars* to within ½ inch of top, wipe
  rims clean and screw on lids.

- Place jars in water bath** to cover and heat
  in boiling water for at least 10 minutes.
  Cool before tightening lids completely.
  Makes about 7 pints.

*Page 8: Instructions for sterilizing jars and lids.
**Page 8-10: Instructions for water bath.

Mild Pepper Sauce

2 - 2½ pounds tomatoes, peeled, minced
½ pound dried sweet red chile peppers
    or 1 pound poblano or ancho peppers
1 medium white onion, minced
½ teaspoon pickling salt
¼ teaspoon oregano
¼ teaspoon sugar

- Peel and chop enough tomatoes to equal
  2 cups minced. Boil peppers in 1 cup water
  until tender, remove from heat and mash
  through sieve. Mix with tomatoes, onion,
  pickling salt, oregano and sugar and add to
  saucepan; boil until tender.

- Pour into hot sterilized jars* to within
  ½ inch of top, wipe rims clean and screw
  on lids.

- Place jars in water bath** to cover and heat
  in boiling water for at least 10 minutes.
  Cool before tightening lids completely.
  Makes about 3 (½ pint) jars.

*Page 8: Instructions for sterilizing jars and lids.
**Page 8-10: Instructions for water bath.

Homemade Plum Jelly

6 - 6½ pounds ripe plums, peeled, pitted
1 (1.7 ounce) box fruit pectin
7 cups sugar

- Cover plums with water and boil for 15 to 20 minutes. Mash enough plums through strainer or sieve to equal 5 cups strained juice. Pour into saucepan with pectin and bring to rolling boil.

- Add sugar, bring back to a rolling boil and cook for 5 minutes, stirring constantly. Skim foam and pour into hot sterilized jars* to within ½ inch of top, wipe rims clean and screw on lids.

- Place jars in water bath** to cover and heat in boiling water for at least 10 minutes. Cool before tightening lids completely. Makes about 8 to 10 pints.

*Page 8: Instructions for sterilizing jars and lids.
**Page 8-10: Instructions for water bath.

Easy Plum Sauce

This is great with chicken, turkey or pork.

½ - 1 large white onion, minced
4 pounds plums, peeled, pitted
2 tablespoons canned, chopped green chilies
1 clove garlic
1 (1 inch) piece fresh ginger
2 tablespoons mustard seed
1 cup cider vinegar
1 cup white vinegar
2 cups packed brown sugar

- Prepare enough minced onion to equal
  ¾ cup. Puree plums, onions, green chilies,
  garlic, ginger and mustard seed in food
  processor or blender. Combine vinegars and
  brown sugar in large saucepan, bring to a
  gentle boil and reduce heat; stir frequently.

- Pour plum mixture into saucepan and cook
  about 1½ hours or until thick and syrupy.
  into hot sterilized jars* to within ½ inch of
  top, wipe rims clean and screw on lids.

- Place jars in water bath** to cover and heat
  in boiling water for at least 10 minutes.
  Cool before tightening lids completely.
  Makes about 4 pints.

*Page 8: Instructions for sterilizing jars and lids.
**Page 8-10: Instructions for water bath.

Rhubarb Jam

5 - 7 medium-large stalks rhubarb
3 cups sugar
1 (6 ounce) package strawberry gelatin

- Finely chop enough rhubarb to equal 4 cups. Combine with sugar and ½ cup water in large saucepan and gently boil until tender; stir frequently. Remove from heat, add gelatin and stir well.

- Pour into hot sterilized jars* to within ½ inch of top, wipe rims clean and screw on lids.

- Place jars in water bath** to cover and heat in boiling water for at least 10 minutes. Cool before tightening lids completely. Makes about 4 pints.

*Page 8: Instructions for sterilizing jars and lids.
**Page 8-10: Instructions for water bath.

If your jam is too thick, it may
be the result of cooking too long at a
temperature that is too low or it may
be an indication of not enough stirring.

Pickled Summer Squash

4 pounds summer squash
3 large onions
1 cup vinegar
1¾ cups sugar
½ cup chopped green bell pepper
½ teaspoon mustard seed
½ teaspoon celery seed

- Prepare enough sliced or whole squash to equal 8 cups and enough sliced onions to equal 2 cups.

- Add all ingredients, except squash, to large saucepan and bring to a rolling boil. Add squash and boil for 1 minute.

- Pour into hot sterilized jars* to within ½ inch of top, wipe rims clean and screw on lids.

- Place jars in water bath** to cover and heat in boiling water for at least 10 minutes. Cool before tightening lids completely. Makes about 7 pints.

*Page 8: Instructions for sterilizing jars and lids.
**Page 8-10: Instructions for water bath.

Squash Pickles

1½ - 2 pounds yellow squash
Pickling salt
3 cups sugar
2 cups vinegar
2 teaspoons mustard seed
2 teaspoons celery seed
2 cups (about 3 whole) chopped red bell
    peppers
2 cups (about 3 whole) chopped green bell
    peppers
2 large onions, thinly sliced in rings

- Slice enough squash to equal 3 cups and
  place in salted ice water; let stand for 1 hour
  and drain well. Combine sugar, vinegar and
  seasonings in large saucepan and bring to a
  boil. Add squash and remaining vegetables
  and boil for 5 minutes.

- Pour into hot sterilized jars* to within ½ inch
  of top, wipe rims clean and screw on lids.

- Place jars in water bath** to cover and heat
  in boiling water for at least 10 minutes.
  Cool before tightening lids completely.
  Makes about 3 to 4 pints.

*Page 8: Instructions for sterilizing jars and lids.
**Page 8-10: Instructions for water bath.

Easy Strawberry Preserves

2 (1 quart) cartons strawberries, stemmed
7 cups sugar
1 teaspoon Epsom salt

- Finely chop enough strawberries to equal
  4 cups and pour into large saucepan. Add
  sugar and Epsom salt, stir frequently, cook
  over medium heat for about 10 minutes;
  stir frequently.

- Skim foam off top. Pour into hot sterilized
  jars* to within ½ inch of top, wipe rims
  clean and screw on lids.

- Place jars in water bath** to cover and heat
  in boiling water for at least 10 minutes.
  Cool before tightening lids completely.
  Makes about 4 pints.

*Page 8: Instructions for sterilizing jars and lids.
**Page 8-10: Instructions for water bath.

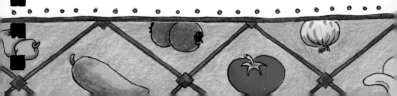

Special Strawberry-Fig Jam

1 - 1½ pounds figs, stems trimmed
3 cups sugar
2 (6 ounce) packages strawberry gelatin
4 drops red food coloring

- Finely chop enough figs to equal 3 cups. Pour into saucepan, add sugar and cook until figs are tender. Add gelatin and stir until it dissolves.

- Pour into hot sterilized jars* to within ½ inch of top, wipe rims clean and screw on lids.

- Place jars in water bath** to cover and heat in boiling water for at least 10 minutes. Cool before tightening lids completely. Makes about 4 pints.

*Page 8: Instructions for sterilizing jars and lids.
**Page 8-10: Instructions for water bath.

Easy Ice Box Strawberry Jam

1 (1 pint) carton strawberries, sliced
¼ cup honey
¼ teaspoon finely grated lemon peel

- Place all ingredients in saucepan and bring to a boil. Simmer over medium-low heat, stirring occasionally for about 40 minutes until mixture thickens.

- Pour into clean jars to within ½ inch of top, screw on lid and refrigerate. Makes about 2 cups or 1 pint.

The son of a farmer joined the army. On his first trip home after basic training, his father asked him, "How's army life?" His son replied, "Real good. The food is good, the work is easy and they let you sleep real late in the morning."

Easy Cold-Packed Tomatoes

Fresh tomatoes

- Peel or blanch tomatoes to remove skins. Pack whole or quartered tomatoes into hot sterilized jars* to within ½ inch of top, wipe rims clean and screw on lids.

- Place jars in water bath** to cover and heat in boiling water for 35 minutes for pint jars and 45 minutes for quart jars. Cool before tightening lids completely.

TIP: 1 medium tomato equals about 1 cup chopped. 2 cups equal 1 pint.

TIP: After opening, store jars in refrigerator.

*Page 8: Instructions for sterilizing jars and lids.
**Page 8-10: Instructions for water bath.

How do you fix a broken tomato?
Tomato paste

Pick of
the Crop

Easy
Hot-Packed
Tomatoes

Fresh ripe tomatoes

- Peel or blanch tomatoes to remove skins.
  Cut in wedges or leave whole and place in
  large saucepan. Gently boil tomatoes for
  5 minutes with just enough water to cover.

- Place tomatoes into hot sterilized jars* and
  pour liquid to within ½ inch of top, wipe
  rims clean and screw on lids.

- Place jars in water bath** to cover and heat
  in boiling water for at least 10 minutes for
  pint jars and 15 minutes for quart jars.
  Cool before tightening lids completely.

*Page 8: Instructions for sterilizing jars and lids.
**Page 8-10: Instructions for water bath.

What vegetable did Noah leave off
the Ark?

Leeks.

Tomato-Okra Mix

Okra
Tomatoes
Pickling salt

- Trim ends off okra and slice; scald tomatoes in boiling to remove peel, quarter or leave whole. Pack into hot sterilized jars* to within ½ inch of top, add ½ teaspoon pickling salt for 1 pint and 1 teaspoon pickling salt for 1 quart jar, wipe rims clean and screw on lids.

- Place jars in water bath** to cover and heat in boiling water for at least 35 minutes for pint jars and 45 minutes for quart jars (Add water if necessary. Bring back to rapid boil and reset timer to entire processing time.) Cool before tightening lids completely.

*Page 8: Instructions for sterilizing jars and lids.
**Page 8-10: Instructions for water bath.

My mother's menu consisted of two things: take it or leave it.
—Buddy Hackett

Tomato Preserves

5 pounds ripe tomatoes
8 cups sugar
2 lemons, thinly sliced

- Dip tomatoes in boiling water, peel and let stand overnight. Drain juice into saucepan, add sugar and boil rapidly until mixture spins a thread.

- Add tomatoes and lemons and boil until thick and clear. Pour into hot sterilized jars* to within ½ inch of top, wipe rims clean and screw on lids.

- Place jars in water bath** to cover and heat in boiling water for at least 10 minutes. Cool before tightening lids completely. Makes about 6 pints.

*Page 8: Instructions for sterilizing jars and lids.
**Page 8-10: Instructions for water bath.

What do you call a sleeping bull?
A bulldozer.

Steve Cukrov/Shutterstock.com

Chunky Salsa

6 pounds tomatoes, blanched, peeled, minced*
2 green bell peppers, cored, seeded, minced
2 red bell peppers, cored, seeded, minced
3 white onions, minced
1 large bunch cilantro, snipped
2 (7 ounce) cans diced green chilies with liquid
2 - 3 tablespoons minced garlic
1 tablespoon ground cumin
3 cups (5% acidity) apple cider vinegar
¾ cup lime juice
1½ teaspoons pickling salt

- Combine all ingredients in large saucepan and bring to a boil. Reduce heat and simmer for 10 minutes. Pour into hot sterilized jars** to within ½ inch of top, wipe rims clean and screw on lids.

- Place jars in water bath*** to cover and heat in boiling water for at least 10 minutes. Cool before tightening lids completely. Makes about 9 pints.

*TIP: Blanch tomatoes by dipping in boiling water for a few seconds; then dip in cold water to slip skins off.

**Page 8: Instructions for sterilizing jars and lids.
***Page 8-10: Instructions for water bath.

Backyard Barbecue Sauce

1 cup tomato ketchup
¾ cup packed brown sugar
½ cup corn oil (not other vegetable oil)
¼ cup vinegar
3 tablespoons Worcestershire sauce
¼ cup chili powder
1 tablespoon prepared mustard

- Combine all ingredients and stir well. Pour into hot sterilized pint jar* to within ½ inch of top, wipe rim clean and screw on lid.

- Place jar in water bath** to cover and heat in boiling water for at least 10 minutes. Cool before tightening lid completely. Makes about 1 pint.

*Page 8: Instructions for sterilizing jars and lids.
**Page 8-10: Instructions for water bath.

> Underripe fruit will make jelly too thick and overripe fruit will make jelly too runny.

Grandma's Secret Barbecue Sauce

1 cup white vinegar
½ cup sugar
3 (32 ounce) cans tomato sauce
3 (28 ounce) cans whole tomatoes, pureed
3 large onions, minced
1 pound jalapenos, seeded, chopped
5 - 7 cloves garlic, minced
1 tablespoon pickling salt

- Combine vinegar, sugar, tomato sauce and pureed tomatoes in saucepan with 1 cup water and pickling salt; bring to a boil. Add remaining ingredients.

- Cook on medium for 30 to 45 minutes; stir continuously to prevent scorching or sticking. Pour into hot sterilized jars* to within ½ inch of top, wipe rims clean and screw on lids.

- Place jars in water bath** to cover and heat in boiling water for at least 10 minutes. Cool before tightening lids completely. Makes about 10 to 12 pints.

*Page 8: Instructions for sterilizing jars and lids.
**Page 8-10: Instructions for water bath.

Old-Fashioned Chili Sauce

6½ pounds ripe tomatoes, diced
½ - 1 large white onion, minced
1½ cups sugar
1 teaspoon nutmeg
¾ teaspoon hot pepper sauce
½ teaspoon curry powder
2 cups vinegar
2 teaspoons ginger
1 teaspoon cinnamon
1 teaspoon dry mustard
5 teaspoons pickling salt

- Prepare enough pureed tomatoes to equal 4 quarts and enough minced onion to equal ⅔ cup. Add all ingredients to large saucepan and gently boil for 2 hours; stir frequently to prevent scorching.

- Pour into hot sterilized jars* to within ½ inch of top, wipe rims clean and screw on lids.

- Place jars in water bath** to cover and heat in boiling water for at least 30 minutes. Cool before tightening lids completely. Makes about 4 to 6 quarts or 8 to 12 pints.

*Page 8: Instructions for sterilizing jars and lids.
**Page 8-10: Instructions for water bath.

Pick of the Crop

Hot Chihuahua Picante Sauce

4 quarts (about 24) ripe tomatoes, peeled,
    cored, chopped
2 - 2½ large white onions, minced
6 - 8 medium jalapenos, seeded, minced
1 cup sugar
2½ cups vinegar
3 tablespoons pickling salt

- Prepare enough chopped tomatoes to equal
  4 quarts, enough minced onions to equal
  2 cups and enough minced jalapenos to
  equal 1 to 1½ cups.

- Combine all ingredients in large saucepan,
  cook on low for about 45 minutes; stir
  frequently. Pour into hot sterilized jars* to
  within ½ inch of top, wipe rims clean and
  screw on lids.

- Place jars in water bath** to cover and heat
  in boiling water for at least 10 minutes.
  Cool before tightening lids completely.
  Makes about 6 pints.

*Page 8: Instructions for sterilizing jars and lids.
**Page 8-10: Instructions for water bath.

Homemade Ketchup

10 - 15 pounds tomatoes, peeled, pureed
2 cups sugar
1 cup white vinegar
1 tablespoon ground cinnamon
1 tablespoon dry mustard
Red food coloring, optional

- Prepare enough tomato juice to equal 5 quarts. Combine tomatoes, sugar and vinegar in large saucepan. Make seasoning bag out of thin cloth, add spices and close securely.

- Add to saucepan and cook over medium low heat until juice reaches desired consistency. Stir frequently so juice will not stick to bottom of pan.

- Remove seasoning bag and add red food coloring if needed. Pour into hot sterilized jars* to within ½ inch of top, wipe rims clean and screw on lids.

- Place jars in water bath** to cover and heat in boiling water for at least 10 minutes. Cool before tightening lids completely. Makes about 4 quarts.

*Page 8: Instructions for sterilizing jars and lids.
**Page 8-10: Instructions for water bath.

Homemade Vegetable Juice

2 - 3 pounds tomatoes, peeled, pureed
4 ribs celery, pureed
2 bell peppers, cored, seeded, pureed
1 large onion, pureed
1 jalapeno, seeded, pureed, optional

- Puree enough tomatoes to equal 2 quarts tomato juice. Pour into large saucepan with remaining ingredients and bring to a boil. Remove from heat and pour through strainer.

- Cook again until it boils. Pour into hot sterilized jars* to within ½ inch of top, wipe rims clean and screw on lids.

- Place jars in water bath** to cover and heat in boiling water for at least 20 minutes. Cool before tightening lids completely. Makes about 2 to 3 quarts or 4 to 6 pints.

*Page 8: Instructions for sterilizing jars and lids.
**Page 8-10: Instructions for water bath.

What do you call cattle with a sense of humor?

Laughingstock.

Old-Fashioned Chow-Chow

This recipe is more than 100 years old and is still one of the best.

7 - 8 pounds tomatoes, peeled, minced
6 jalapenos, seeded, minced*
12 bell peppers, seeded, minced
12 medium onions, minced
2 large heads cabbage, shredded
¾ cup pickling salt

- Mix vegetables with pickling salt in large bowl and stir well. Set aside for 2 hours and drain well.

6½ cups sugar
2 quarts vinegar
2 teaspoons grated ginger
1 teaspoon ground mustard
1 teaspoon ground cloves
1 teaspoon ground cinnamon
1 teaspoon turmeric
1 teaspoon celery seed

- Mix sugar, vinegar and seasonings, except celery seed, in saucepan and gently boil for

Continued next page...

Continued from previous page...

20 minutes. Add celery seed, stir well and pour over vegetables. Pour into hot sterilized jars* to within ½ inch of top, wipe rims clean and screw on lids.

- Place jars in water bath** to cover and heat in boiling water for at least 10 minutes. Cool before tightening lids completely. Makes about 14 pints.

*TIP: *Wear rubber gloves when handling hot peppers.*

*Page 8: Instructions for sterilizing jars and lids.
**Page 8-10: Instructions for water bath.

Grandma's Secret: Label top of lid with date and contents so you will not use the flat lid again. It is all right to reuse the screw-on ring that tightens the lid

Aunt Eva's Watermelon Rind Pickles

About 7 pounds watermelon rind
1 cup lime juice
1 quart vinegar
5 pounds sugar
6 - 7 cinnamon sticks
1 teaspoon whole cloves
1 teaspoon mace

- Remove all green outer edges and all red inner edges of watermelon rind. Cut into 3-inch pieces and place in large ceramic crock or glass container. Mix lime juice with enough water to cover rind, pour into container and soak rind overnight.

- Mix vinegar, sugar and spices in some water. Rinse rind in cold water, drain and pour vinegar mixture over top. Add enough water to cover rind and soak overnight.

Continued next page...

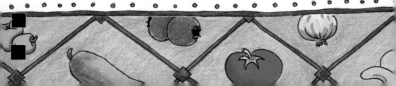

Continued from previous page…

- On third day, cook rind mixture for 20 minutes over low heat. Pour into hot sterilized jars* to within ½ inch of top, wipe rims clean and screw on lids.

- Place jars in water bath** to cover and heat in boiling water for at least 10 minutes. Cool before tightening lids completely. Makes about 6 pints

TIP: If you want to brighten the rinds, add food coloring.

*Page 8: Instructions for sterilizing jars and lids.
**Page 8-10: Instructions for water bath.

Aunt Eva's Watermelon Rind Pickles →

I do not like broccoli. And I haven't liked it since I was a little kid and my mother made me eat it. Now I'm the President of the United States of America and I'm not going to eat broccoli any more."

—President George H.W. Bush, 1990

Zucchini Relish

4 - 4½ pounds zucchini, minced
8 - 10 medium carrots, diced
2 - 3 large white onions, minced
1 - 2 large bell peppers, cored, seeded, diced
2¼ cups white vinegar
¼ cup sugar
2 tablespoons pickling salt
1 tablespoon celery seed
¾ teaspoon dry mustard

- Mince enough zucchini to equal 4 cups, enough diced carrots to equal 3 cups, enough minced onion to equal 3 cups and enough diced bell peppers to equal 1½ cups.

- Mix all ingredients in large skillet. Saute over medium heat for 15 minutes or until tender. Pour into hot sterilized jars* to within ½ inch of top, wipe rims clean and screw on lids.

- Place jars in water bath** to cover and heat in boiling water for at least 10 minutes. Cool before tightening lids completely. Makes about 8 pints.

*Page 8: Instructions for sterilizing jars and lids.
**Page 8-10: Instructions for water bath.

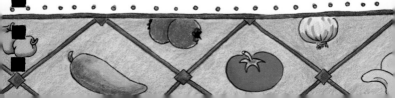

Zucchini-Tomato Medley

Zucchini
Tomatoes
Pickling salt

- Trim ends of zucchini and slice. (Do not peel.) Scald tomatoes in boiling water and remove skin. Quarter or chop tomatoes and pack into sterilized* jars with zucchini to within 1 inch of top. To each pint jar, add ½ teaspoon pickling salt; add 1 teaspoon pickling salt to each quart jar. Wipe rims clean and screw on lids.

- Place jars in water bath** to cover and heat in boiling water for 35 minutes for pint jars and 45 minutes for quart jars and cool before tightening lids completely.

*Page 8: Instructions for sterilizing jars and lids.
**Page 8-10: Instructions for water bath.

End of Garden Canning

When the garden is down to its last hurrah, just put what's left in a jar. You don't lose any produce and you get beautiful jars filled with interesting shapes, sizes and colors of your favorite fruits and vegetables.

Fruits and vegetables
2½ cups vinegar
2 - 3 cloves garlic
¼ cup pickling salt

- Place fruits and vegetables into pint jars. Add vinegar, garlic and pickling salt to 2½ cups water in saucepan, bring to a rolling boil and pour over fruits and vegetables in hot sterilized jars* to within ½ inch of top. Wipe rims clean and screw on lids.

- Place jars in water bath** to cover and heat in boiling water for 35 minutes for pint jars and 45 minutes for quart jars. Cool before tightening lids completely. Makes 2 pints.

*Page 8: Instructions for sterilizing jars and lids.
**Page 8-10: Instructions for water bath.

Bibliography

Ball Blue Book: Guide to Preserving. Altrista
    Consumer Products, 2004.

Ball Complete Book of Home Preserving. Judi Kingry
    and Lauren Devine. Robert Rose, Publisher. 2006.

Complete Guide to Home Canning and Preserving.
    U.S. Department of Agriculture. Revised 2009.
    bnpublishing.net. This can also be viewed and
    downloaded at: www.uga.edu/nchfp/publications/
    publications_usda.html

Food Lover's Companion by Sharon Tyler Herbst.
    Barron's Educational Series, Inc. 2001.

Pickles and Relishes: From Apples to Zucchinis by
    Andrea Chesman, Storey Publishing. 1991.

The Complete Book of Small Batch Preserving. Ellie
    Topp and Margaret Howard. Firefly Books. 2007.

*You Can Can. A Visual Step-by-Step Guide to Canning,
    Preserving and Pickling.* Better Homes and
    Gardens. 2010

Additional References

http://agrilifeextension.tamu.edu
www.ball.com
www.burpee.com
http://freshpreserving.com
www.jarden.com
www.pickyourown.org
http://uga.edu/nchp National Center
    for Home Food Preservation
http://usda.gov

Index

Cookbooks Published by Cookbook Resources, LLC
Bringing Family and Friends to the Table

The Best 1001 Short, Easy Recipes
1001 Slow Cooker Recipes
1001 Short, Easy, Inexpensive Recipes
1001 Fast Easy Recipes
1001 America's Favorite Recipes
1001 Easy Inexpensive Grilling Recipes
Easy Slow Cooker Cookbook
Busy Woman's Slow Cooker Recipes
Busy Woman's Quick & Easy Recipes
365 Easy Soups and Stews
365 Easy Chicken Recipes
365 Easy One-Dish Recipes
365 Easy Soup Recipes
365 Easy Vegetarian Recipes
365 Easy Casserole Recipes
365 Easy Pasta Recipes
365 Easy Slow Cooker Recipes
Super Simple Cupcake Recipes
Leaving Home Cookbook and Survival Guide
Essential 3-4-5 Ingredient Recipes
Ultimate 4 Ingredient Cookbook
Easy Cooking with 5 Ingredients
The Best of Cooking with 3 Ingredients
Easy Diabetic Recipes
Ultimate 4 Ingredient Diabetic Cookbook
4-Ingredient Recipes for 30-Minute Meals
Cooking with Beer
The Washington Cookbook
The Pennsylvania Cookbook
The California Cookbook
Best-Loved New England Recipes
Best-Loved Canadian Recipes
Best-Loved Recipes from the Pacific Northwest
Easy Homemade Preserves (Handbook with Photos)
Garden Fresh Recipes (Handbook with Photos)
Easy Slow Cooker Recipes (Handbook with Photos)

Cool Smoothies (Handbook with Photos)
Easy Cupcake Recipes (Handbook with Photos)
Easy Soup Recipes (Handbook with Photos)
Classic Tex-Mex and Texas Cooking
Best-Loved Southern Recipes
Classic Southwest Cooking
Miss Sadie's Southern Cooking
Classic Pennsylvania Dutch Cooking
The Quilters' Cookbook
Healthy Cooking with 4 Ingredients
Trophy Hunter's Wild Game Cookbook
Recipe Keeper
Simple Old-Fashioned Baking
Quick Fixes with Cake Mixes
Kitchen Keepsakes & More Kitchen Keepsakes
Cookbook 25 Years
Texas Longhorn Cookbook
The Authorized Texas Ranger Cookbook
Gifts for the Cookie Jar
All New Gifts for the Cookie Jar
The Big Bake Sale Cookbook
Easy One-Dish Meals
Easy Potluck Recipes
Easy Casseroles Cookbook
Easy Desserts
Sunday Night Suppers
Easy Church Suppers
365 Easy Meals
Gourmet Cooking with 5 Ingredients
Muffins In A Jar
A Little Taste of Texas
A Little Taste of Texas II
Ultimate Gifts for the Cookie Jar

cookbook resources LLC

www.cookbookresources.com
Toll-Free 866-229-2665
Your Ultimate Source for Easy Cookbooks

cookbook
resources LLC
www.cookbookresources.com
Toll-Free 866-229-2665
Your Ultimate Source for Easy Cookbooks